Gabon Unveiled:
The Coup of 2023

John David

Introduction:

In the heart of Central Africa lies a nation of vibrant landscapes, rich cultural diversity, and a tumultuous political history. Gabon, a country endowed with breathtaking natural beauty and abundant resources, has often found itself at the crossroads of progress and unrest. This book delves deep into the complex tapestry of Gabon, unveiling the pages of its history, the significance of its unique biodiversity, the intricacies of its oil production, the challenges it faces, and a pivotal event that shook the nation in 2023—the coup that reshaped its destiny.

Gabon, known for its lush rainforests, pristine coastlines, and diverse wildlife, has captivated explorers and scientists for centuries. Yet, beneath the surface of this natural wonderland lies a story of political intrigue, economic aspirations, and the aspirations of its people. From its early days as a French colony to its struggle for independence,

Gabon's journey to nationhood has been marked by resilience and transformation.

This book embarks on a journey through the annals of Gabon's past, shedding light on its political stability, regional diplomacy, cultural diversity, and contributions to literature and the arts. It unravels the intricacies of its oil-dependent economy, the challenges of development, and the persistent efforts to conserve its unique biodiversity.

At the heart of this narrative stands the coup of 2023—a moment that shook the foundations of Gabonese society. We will explore the events that led to this pivotal juncture, the motivations of those who sought to reshape the nation's destiny, and the consequences that reverberated far beyond its borders.

As we navigate the pages of Gabon's story, we will encounter a nation striving to find its place in the world, wrestling with the complexities of democracy, governance, and the pursuit of prosperity for all its citizens. Through the lens of history, politics, culture, and society, we will uncover the multifaceted tapestry of a nation that continues to evolve and shape its future in the heart of Africa.

Join us on this journey as we unveil the captivating narrative of Gabon—its past, present, and the indomitable spirit that propels it forward.

Chapter 1

Overview

- Background and significance of Gabon
- Overview of political history

-Background and significance of Gabon:

Geography and Demographics:
 Gabon is situated on the west coast of Central Africa, bordered by the Atlantic Ocean to the west and surrounded by Equatorial Guinea, Cameroon, and the Republic of the Congo. Its diverse landscape includes rainforests, savannas, and coastal areas. The capital city is Libreville. Gabon's population is composed of various ethnic groups, with the Fang being the largest. French is the official language.

Colonial History:
 Gabon was a French colony for much of its history. It was first explored by Portuguese navigators in

the 15th century and later came under French control in the late 19th century. It was part of French Equatorial Africa until it gained autonomy in 1958.

Independence and Political Evolution:
Gabon became an independent nation on August 17, 1960, with Léon M'ba as its first president. After his death, his vice president, Albert-Bernard Bongo, assumed power in 1967. Bongo ruled Gabon for over four decades, creating a political dynasty that continues to influence the country's politics. Bongo's rule was marked by relative political stability compared to some of its neighboring countries.

Economic Factors:
Gabon's economy has historically relied heavily on oil exports, which became a significant factor after oil was discovered offshore in the 1970s. While oil production brought in revenue, it also made the country vulnerable to fluctuations in global oil prices. Efforts have been made to diversify the economy, with a focus on mining, forestry, and other sectors.

Social and Cultural Landscape:
Gabon is known for its rich cultural diversity. The Fang people, particularly the Myene sub-group, have a significant influence on Gabonese culture. Traditional practices, music, dance, and art continue to be an integral part of the Gabonese

way of life. The country's cultural expressions have also influenced African literature and arts.

Political Governance:
 Gabon's political scene has been dominated by the Bongo family. After Albert-Bernard Bongo's death in 2009, his son Ali Bongo Ondimba took over the presidency. This dynastic rule has been both a source of stability and contention in the country's political landscape.

Environmental Conservation:
 Gabon's rainforests are part of the Congo Basin, one of the world's largest tropical rainforest areas. Recognizing the ecological importance of its forests, Gabon has implemented measures to protect its natural heritage, establishing national parks and adopting sustainable forestry practices.

Diplomatic Role:
 Gabon has been an active participant in regional and international diplomacy. It has hosted several high-profile international events, including the New York Forum Africa, aimed at fostering dialogue on economic development and investment in Africa.

Challenges and Prospects:
 Despite its resource wealth and relative stability, Gabon faces challenges including income inequality, governance concerns, and economic diversification. The need to balance economic growth with environmental conservation and

address social issues remains crucial for the country's development.

Ethnic Diversity:
 Gabon is home to a mosaic of ethnic groups, each with its own languages, traditions, and cultural practices. In addition to the Fang, other prominent ethnic groups include the Bapounou, Eshira, and Mpongwe. This diversity contributes to Gabon's rich cultural tapestry and influences its social dynamics.

Colonial Legacy:
 During the colonial period, Gabon served as a French trading post and later became part of French Equatorial Africa. The legacy of colonialism has left an imprint on various aspects of Gabonese society, from language and education to administrative structures.

Education and Literacy:
 Gabon has invested in education, resulting in relatively high literacy rates compared to some of its neighbors. The country has universities and educational institutions that contribute to the development of skilled human resources.

Traditional Beliefs and Religions:
 While Christianity is the predominant religion in Gabon, traditional animist beliefs still hold significance for many Gabonese people. These

beliefs are often intertwined with daily life and cultural practices, influencing ceremonies, rituals, and social interactions.

Art and Music:
 Gabonese art and music play an essential role in cultural expression. Traditional instruments like the mvet (a type of harp) and ngombi (a stringed instrument) are used in various ceremonies and performances. Music and dance serve as a means of communication, storytelling, and preserving cultural heritage.

Cultural Festivals:
 Gabon's cultural calendar is punctuated by various festivals that celebrate its heritage. The "Ngondo" festival of the Fang people and the "Makina" festival of the Bapounou are examples of events that showcase traditional dances, rituals, and communal gatherings.

Urbanization and Rural Life:
 While urbanization is on the rise, a significant portion of Gabon's population still resides in rural areas, where traditional ways of life persist. Urban centers like Libreville have experienced growth and modernization, leading to changes in lifestyle and social structures.

Healthcare and Infrastructure:
 Gabon has made efforts to improve healthcare services and infrastructure, particularly in urban

areas. However, challenges such as access to healthcare in remote regions and addressing health disparities remain.

Language Diversity:
 In addition to French, many indigenous languages are spoken in Gabon. These languages contribute to the country's linguistic richness and cultural diversity, serving as a means of preserving traditional knowledge and identity.

Women's Role in Society:
 The role of women in Gabonese society has evolved over time. While women traditionally played key roles in family and community life, modernization has brought changes in gender roles and expectations. Efforts have been made to promote gender equality and empower women in various sectors.

 Gabon's background is characterized by its ethnic diversity, colonial history, cultural heritage, traditional beliefs, and modern development. The country's unique blend of past and present contributes to its distinct identity within the African continent.

SIGNIFICANCE OF GABON:

1. **Biodiversity and Conservation**: Gabon is renowned for its rich biodiversity and extensive

rainforests, which are home to a diverse range of flora and fauna. It has made efforts to preserve its natural heritage through the creation of national parks and conservation initiatlves.

Biodiversity Riches:
 Gabon boasts one of the most biodiverse landscapes in Africa. Its rainforests are part of the Congo Basin, one of the world's most important biodiversity hotspots. The country's diverse ecosystems include tropical rainforests, wetlands, savannas, rivers, and coastal areas, fostering a wide range of plant and animal species.

Flora and Fauna:
 Gabon's forests are home to an astonishing variety of plant species, including numerous endemic species found nowhere else on Earth. The forests provide habitat for an array of wildlife, such as forest elephants, gorillas, chimpanzees, mandrills, and a rich diversity of bird species.

National Parks and Protected Areas:
 To safeguard its natural heritage, Gabon has established a network of national parks and protected areas. Some notable parks include Ivindo National Park, Loango National Park, and Lopé National Park. These areas not only protect biodiversity but also provide opportunities for eco-tourism and scientific research.

Conservation Initiatives:

Gabon has demonstrated a commitment to conservation through various initiatives. The government has set ambitious goals for preserving its forests and biodiversity. The Gabonese National Parks Agency (ANPN) is responsible for managing protected areas and implementing conservation policies.

Gabon Bleu Initiative:
Launched in 2019, the Gabon Bleu Initiative aims to protect and preserve marine ecosystems along the country's coastline. This initiative recognizes the importance of marine biodiversity and sustainable fisheries for Gabon's economy and ecosystem health.

Eco-Tourism and Research:
Gabon's pristine natural landscapes attract researchers, scientists, and tourists interested in exploring its biodiversity. Eco-tourism activities, such as gorilla tracking and birdwatching, provide opportunities for visitors to appreciate the country's flora and fauna while contributing to conservation efforts.

Challenges and Threats:
Despite its commitment to conservation, Gabon faces challenges that threaten its biodiversity. Illegal logging, poaching, habitat loss due to infrastructure development, and climate change are among the threats that need to be addressed to ensure the long-term survival of its ecosystems.

International Recognition:
 Gabon's efforts in conservation have gained international recognition. It has received support from international organizations, such as the World Wildlife Fund (WWF) and the United Nations, for its conservation initiatives and commitment to sustainable development.

Economic and Environmental Balance:
 Gabon faces the challenge of balancing economic development with environmental protection. The reliance on oil exports and the desire to diversify the economy while conserving its natural resources present complex policy considerations.

Global Conservation Impact:
 Given the global significance of Gabon's biodiversity, its conservation efforts contribute not only to safeguarding local ecosystems but also to global biodiversity conservation and climate change mitigation efforts.

In summary, Gabon's rich biodiversity and commitment to conservation make it a critical player in preserving the Congo Basin's unique ecosystems. Its efforts contribute to the broader global agenda of protecting biodiversity and addressing environmental challenges.

2. **Oil Production**: Gabon is one of Africa's major oil producers. Oil exports contribute significantly to its economy, making it a key player in global energy markets. However, this heavy reliance on oil also poses economic challenges due to fluctuating oil prices.

Oil Reserves and Production:
 Gabon is one of Africa's significant oil producers. Oil was discovered off its coast in the 1970s, leading to the development of the petroleum sector. The country's proven oil reserves are primarily located offshore in the Atlantic Ocean.

Economic Impact:
 Oil has historically been a crucial driver of Gabon's economy, contributing a substantial portion of its government revenue and foreign exchange earnings. The revenue generated from oil exports has funded infrastructure development, social programs, and public services.

Dependency on Oil:
 Gabon's heavy reliance on oil exports has implications for its economic stability. The economy is vulnerable to fluctuations in global oil prices, which can impact government revenues and budget planning. Low oil prices can strain public finances and hinder development efforts.

Diversification Efforts:

Recognizing the risks of over-dependency on oil, Gabon has undertaken efforts to diversify its economy. Initiatives to promote sectors like mining, agriculture, forestry, and tourism are aimed at reducing the country's vulnerability to oil price shocks.

Foreign Investment and Partnerships:
The development of Gabon's oil sector has been facilitated by partnerships with international oil companies. Foreign direct investment and collaboration with multinational corporations have contributed to the exploration, production, and export of oil.

Environmental Concerns:
Oil production can have environmental impacts, including risks of oil spills and habitat disruption. Balancing the economic benefits of oil production with environmental conservation is a challenge that Gabon, like many oil-producing nations, faces.

Sustainability and Governance:
Efforts to ensure sustainable oil production involve adopting environmentally responsible practices, regulating exploration and production activities, and implementing transparency and good governance measures to manage revenues effectively.

Local Communities and Social Impact:
Oil production can have both positive and negative impacts on local communities. While it can provide

job opportunities and infrastructure development, there can also be social disruptions, environmental degradation, and challenges related to managing oil revenues for the benefit of all citizens.

Infrastructure Development:
 The oil sector has driven the development of essential infrastructure, including ports, pipelines, and processing facilities. These infrastructural investments have contributed to the country's connectivity and economic growth.

Future Prospects:
 As global trends shift towards renewable energy and environmental sustainability, Gabon faces questions about the long-term viability of its oil-dependent economy. Diversifying the economy, investing in renewable energy sources, and adopting innovative technologies could play a role in shaping its future.

Global Energy Dynamics:
 Gabon's role in global energy markets is influenced by factors such as global oil demand, geopolitical events, technological advancements, and efforts to reduce greenhouse gas emissions. The country's oil production decisions can have implications beyond its borders.

Exploration and Offshore Operations:

The majority of Gabon's oil reserves are located offshore in deepwater fields. Exploration and drilling activities are conducted by multinational oil companies using advanced technologies to access these reserves located beneath the ocean floor.

Production and Export:
Gabon's oil production involves extracting crude oil from beneath the sea floor and transporting it to onshore processing facilities. The processed crude oil is then exported to international markets, primarily through tanker shipments.

Oil Fields and Infrastructure:
Major oil fields in Gabon include Rabi-Kounga, Mandji, and many others. Infrastructure such as drilling platforms, pipelines, and storage tanks are essential components of the oil production process.

Joint Ventures and Contracts:
Oil production in Gabon often involves joint ventures between the government and international oil companies. These agreements outline the terms of exploration, production, revenue sharing, and environmental responsibility.

Economic Impact:
Oil revenue has historically been a crucial source of income for Gabon. It has funded infrastructure projects, public services, and social programs. Economic growth and development have been closely tied to the fortunes of the oil sector.

Oil Price Volatility:
 Global oil prices are subject to fluctuations influenced by geopolitical events, supply and demand dynamics, and global economic conditions. This volatility can impact Gabon's fiscal planning and economic stability.

Revenue Management:
 Managing oil revenues effectively is a challenge for oil-producing nations. Gabon, like others, must strike a balance between current spending and saving for the future through mechanisms like sovereign wealth funds.

Sustainability and Environmental Concerns:
 Oil production can have environmental impacts, including potential oil spills, ecosystem disruption, and carbon emissions. Mitigating these impacts requires robust regulatory frameworks and adherence to environmental standards.

Local Content Development:
 Efforts to enhance the local content in the oil sector involve promoting the participation of Gabonese individuals and businesses in the industry. This can lead to skills development, job creation, and increased economic benefits for local communities.

Stakeholder Engagement:

Effective communication and collaboration between the government, oil companies, and local communities are crucial for ensuring that the benefits of oil production are shared, environmental concerns are addressed, and social impacts are minimized.

Technology and Innovation:
Advancements in oil production technologies, such as enhanced oil recovery techniques, play a role in optimizing the extraction of oil reserves and extending the lifespan of oil fields.

Future Prospects and Diversification:
As global energy transitions gather momentum, Gabon faces the challenge of diversifying its economy away from heavy reliance on oil. Developing renewable energy sources, improving other sectors, and attracting investment are strategies being considered.

Global Trends and Energy Transition:
The world's shift towards renewable energy and climate change mitigation may impact the demand for fossil fuels, including oil. This necessitates strategic planning to ensure economic resilience in the face of changing energy dynamics.

oil production has been a cornerstone of Gabon's economy, driving economic growth and development. However, the country faces the challenge of managing the economic, environmental, and social implications of oil production while preparing for a future marked by global energy transitions.

In summary, oil production has played a pivotal role in Gabon's economic development, government revenues, and infrastructure growth. However, the country is actively considering ways to balance the benefits of oil with sustainable economic diversification and environmental preservation in an evolving global energy landscape.

3. **Political Stability**: Relative political stability has been a hallmark of Gabon compared to some of its neighboring countries. The Bongo family has dominated Gabonese politics for decades, leading to a unique political landscape that has maintained a certain level of stability.

Bongo Dynasty and Political Continuity:
Gabon has experienced a unique political landscape characterized by the long-standing rule of the Bongo family. Omar Bongo, who took power in 1967, ruled for over four decades until his death in 2009. His son, Ali Bongo Ondimba, succeeded him, continuing the family's political legacy.

Stability through Transitions:
Despite changes in leadership, Gabon has managed to maintain relative political stability. Transitions of power have occurred without

widespread violence or major upheaval, a factor that distinguishes Gabon from some other African countries.

Ruling Party Dominance:
 The Gabonese Democratic Party (Parti Démocratique Gabonais, PDG) has been the dominant political party for decades. The party's strong presence in the political landscape has contributed to continuity in governance and policymaking.

State-Controlled Economy:
 Gabon's economy has been characterized by state control and involvement. The government's role in sectors such as oil, forestry, and mining has contributed to a certain level of stability and control over key economic resources.

Social Welfare Programs:
 The government has implemented social welfare programs aimed at improving the lives of citizens. These programs, including education and healthcare initiatives, have contributed to social stability and support for the ruling regime.

Patronage and Political Networks:
 The Bongo family's ability to maintain political stability has been linked to a system of patronage and networks of political allies. This has helped secure support from various segments of society and maintain a degree of control.

Limited Political Pluralism:
 While Gabon has held multi-party elections, the political landscape has often been criticized for limited opposition space. The dominance of the ruling party has sometimes led to allegations of restricted political freedoms.

Ethnic and Regional Dynamics:
 Gabon's ethnic and regional diversity has been managed through a power-sharing model that seeks to maintain a delicate balance among various groups. This approach has contributed to stability by preventing the dominance of a single ethnic or regional faction.

Youth and Aspirations:
 As Gabon's population grows and younger generations become more politically aware, there's an increasing focus on addressing youth aspirations and concerns. Engaging the youth in meaningful ways is crucial for sustaining political stability.

Challenges to Stability:
 While Gabon has enjoyed political stability, challenges such as economic diversification, corruption, inequality, and demands for greater political inclusivity remain. Managing these challenges will be essential for maintaining stability in the long term.

Regional and International Relations:
 Gabon has played a role in regional diplomacy and has been seen as a relatively stable player in the Central African region. The country's involvement in regional organizations and peacekeeping efforts contributes to its stability.

Democratic Governance Debate:
 The stability under the Bongo family has led to debates about the nature of democracy and governance in Gabon. Discussions around term limits, political freedoms, and the balance between stability and change are ongoing.

Historical Context:
 Gabon's political stability can be traced back to its relatively peaceful transition to independence from France in 1960. Unlike some of its neighbors, the country did not experience protracted conflicts or civil wars during this period.

Legacy of Omar Bongo:
 Omar Bongo's lengthy rule, from 1967 to 2009, established a sense of continuity and stability. His ability to navigate regional and international dynamics while maintaining domestic order contributed to the perception of Gabon as a stable nation.

Ethnic Balancing Act:
 Gabon's political stability is partly attributed to the government's efforts to manage ethnic and regional

tensions. The Bongo regime practiced a form of power-sharing that aimed to prevent the dominance of any single ethnic or regional group.

Youth Engagement:
The Bongo family's emphasis on engaging and incorporating young people into governance structures has contributed to social stability. Youth-oriented policies, including educational opportunities and youth councils, have aimed to address the aspirations of the younger generation.

Economic Reforms:
Efforts to diversify the economy beyond oil have been a focus of the government. Economic stability and growth contribute to overall political stability, as a strong economy can help mitigate social unrest and discontent.

Military and Security Forces:
The Gabonese military and security forces have generally remained loyal to the government, contributing to internal stability. While the military has occasionally been involved in political affairs, it has not posed a significant threat to the regime's stability.

Balancing Act: Democracy and Stability:
The balance between democratic governance and political stability is a delicate one. While Gabon has held elections, debates exist about the extent of

political pluralism and the level of opposition space allowed.

Opposition Dynamics:
 Gabon's opposition has faced challenges in forming cohesive alliances or presenting unified alternatives. Internal divisions within opposition parties have sometimes limited their ability to challenge the ruling party effectively.

Post-Election Dynamics:
 Elections, particularly presidential elections, have occasionally sparked post-election disputes and protests. These events underscore the complexity of maintaining political stability while ensuring transparent and credible electoral processes.

Youth Mobilization and Protests:
 In recent years, there have been instances of youth-led protests and calls for greater political participation. The emergence of a more politically conscious and vocal youth population poses both opportunities and challenges for the government.

Media and Freedom of Expression:
 While there is some degree of media freedom in Gabon, concerns have been raised about restrictions on journalists and media outlets critical of the government. Balancing media freedoms with stability and security concerns is an ongoing challenge.

International Relations:
 Gabon's role in regional and international organizations, such as the African Union, has contributed to its image as a responsible actor in global politics. Diplomatic engagement has often been a tool for enhancing the country's stability and influence.

Future Considerations:
 The passing of power from Omar Bongo to his son, Ali Bongo Ondimba, marked a critical juncture. The ongoing challenge for Gabon is to maintain political stability while addressing demands for political reforms, economic diversification, and social development.

In summary, Gabon's political stability is marked by the Bongo family's enduring presence, a dominant ruling party, careful management of ethnic and regional dynamics, and a focus on social welfare. However, the challenges of maintaining this stability amidst evolving economic, social, and political demands are a central consideration for the country's future.

Gabon's political stability is a product of historical legacies, ethnic balancing, economic strategies, engagement with youth, and careful management of opposition dynamics. Maintaining this stability amidst changing domestic and global contexts requires a delicate balance between continuity and responsiveness to evolving aspirations.

4. **Regional Diplomacy**: Gabon has played an active role in regional and international diplomacy, often acting as a mediator in regional conflicts and hosting international events. Its diplomatic efforts have contributed to its positive image on the global stage.

Certainly, here's more insight into Gabon's regional diplomacy:

Mediation and Conflict Resolution:
 Gabon has played a role in regional diplomacy by mediating conflicts and disputes among neighboring countries. Its relatively stable political environment and diplomatic neutrality have positioned it as a potential mediator in conflicts in Central Africa.

Peacekeeping and Stability:
 Gabon has contributed troops to international peacekeeping missions under the auspices of organizations like the United Nations. These contributions demonstrate the country's commitment to promoting stability and resolving conflicts in the region.

Economic Partnerships:
 Gabon has engaged in economic partnerships and cooperation agreements with neighboring countries. Initiatives related to trade, infrastructure development, and investment have been aimed at

enhancing regional economic integration and growth.

Election Monitoring:
 Gabon has participated in election monitoring missions in other African countries, contributing to efforts to ensure credible and transparent electoral processes. This role reinforces the country's commitment to democratic values and good governance.

Hosting International Events:
 Gabon's capital, Libreville, has hosted various international events, conferences, and forums. These gatherings provide platforms for diplomatic discussions, regional cooperation, and the exchange of ideas on issues of mutual interest.

African Union and ECOWAS Engagement:
 Gabon is an active participant in the African Union (AU) and the Economic Community of Central African States (ECCAS). Its engagement in regional organizations allows it to collaborate on matters of regional security, economic development, and governance.

Maritime Security Cooperation:
 Given its coastal location, Gabon has been involved in initiatives to enhance maritime security in the Gulf of Guinea region. Collaborative efforts with neighboring countries aim to combat piracy, illegal fishing, and other maritime threats.

Environmental Conservation and Sustainable Development:
 Gabon's efforts in environmental conservation align with regional goals for sustainable development. Sharing best practices, collaborating on conservation strategies, and addressing transboundary environmental challenges are part of Gabon's regional engagement.

Humanitarian Assistance:
 Gabon has provided humanitarian assistance to neighboring countries during times of crisis. This includes offering refuge to displaced populations and contributing to international efforts to address humanitarian emergencies.

Soft Power Diplomacy:
 Cultural exchanges, educational collaborations, and people-to-people interactions contribute to Gabon's soft power diplomacy. These engagements foster mutual understanding and build relationships that can enhance regional cooperation.

Challenges and Opportunities:
 While Gabon's regional diplomacy efforts have been generally positive, challenges such as resource constraints, political differences, and regional conflicts can impact its effectiveness. Nevertheless, the country's commitment to

diplomacy and stability presents opportunities for continued engagement.

Global Impact of Regional Diplomacy:
 Gabon's involvement in regional diplomacy contributes not only to the stability and development of Central Africa but also to broader continental and international efforts to promote peace, security, and cooperation.

Central African Integration:
Gabon's engagement in regional diplomacy is driven by the goal of promoting integration and collaboration among Central African countries. By participating in regional organizations and initiatives, Gabon aims to strengthen economic ties, enhance security cooperation, and foster shared development objectives.

Transboundary Resources Management:
 Given its geographical location, Gabon is part of various ecosystems and resource networks that span multiple countries. Collaborative efforts to manage transboundary resources, such as waterways and shared forests, are essential for sustainable development and environmental conservation.

Health Diplomacy:
 Gabon's engagement in regional health initiatives has included cooperation on issues such as disease prevention, healthcare capacity-building,

and responses to health emergencies. Collaborative efforts to address health challenges contribute to regional stability and human development.

Infrastructure Connectivity:
Infrastructure projects that improve connectivity between Gabon and neighboring countries, such as road networks and transport corridors, enhance regional trade and economic integration. These projects contribute to the broader goal of strengthening regional ties.

Crisis Response and Humanitarian Aid:
In times of crisis, Gabon has participated in regional efforts to provide humanitarian aid and crisis response. This includes supporting countries facing natural disasters, conflicts, and other emergencies.

Bilateral Relations:
Gabon's diplomatic engagement extends beyond multilateral efforts to include bilateral relations with its neighbors. These diplomatic ties contribute to mutual understanding, economic cooperation, and collaboration on various issues of common interest.

Promotion of Cultural Heritage:
Cultural diplomacy is another facet of Gabon's regional engagement. Through cultural exchanges, festivals, and artistic collaborations, Gabon promotes its cultural heritage and contributes to a

sense of shared identity among Central African nations.

Conflict Prevention and Management:
 Gabon's commitment to conflict prevention and management includes participation in regional mechanisms aimed at maintaining peace and security. By sharing experiences and contributing to peacebuilding efforts, Gabon contributes to regional stability.

Economic Cooperation and Trade:
 Collaborative economic initiatives, such as trade agreements and investment partnerships, contribute to regional economic growth. These efforts can create opportunities for job creation, technology transfer, and shared prosperity.

Alignment with Regional Agendas:
 Gabon's regional diplomacy aligns with broader regional agendas such as the African Union's Agenda 2063 and regional integration initiatives. By participating actively, Gabon helps shape the direction of these agendas and contributes to their implementation.

Dynamic and Evolving Role:
 Gabon's role in regional diplomacy is dynamic and responsive to changing regional dynamics, global challenges, and the evolving needs of Central African countries. As the region faces new

opportunities and obstacles, Gabon's diplomatic engagement continues to adapt.

In summary, Gabon's regional diplomacy efforts extend beyond its borders to address issues of conflict resolution, economic cooperation, environmental conservation, and more. Its role in regional organizations and diplomatic initiatives showcases its commitment to contributing positively to the stability and growth of the Central African region.

5. **Cultural Diversity**: The country is home to a mix of ethnic groups and cultures, each with its own traditions and languages. This diversity has contributed to the country's cultural richness and has been an integral part of its identity.

Ethnic Diversity:
 Gabon is characterized by a rich tapestry of ethnic groups, each with its own unique languages, traditions, and customs. Prominent ethnic groups include the Fang, Eshira, Bapounou, Mpongwe, and many others. This ethnic diversity contributes to the country's cultural richness.

Languages:
 In addition to French, which is the official language, Gabon is home to a multitude of indigenous languages. The linguistic diversity

reflects the country's ethnic mosaic. Languages such as Fang, Myene, Punu, and Nzebi are spoken by various ethnic communities.

Traditional Beliefs:
 While Christianity is the predominant religion in Gabon, traditional animist beliefs still hold significant sway in many communities. These beliefs influence ceremonies, rituals, and daily practices, adding depth to the country's cultural diversity.

Art and Craftsmanship:
 Gabonese art is celebrated for its diversity and intricate designs. Traditional masks, sculptures, and textiles are notable examples of Gabonese craftsmanship. These artistic expressions often carry deep cultural and spiritual significance.

Music and Dance:
 Music and dance are integral to Gabonese culture. Traditional instruments like the mvet (a harp-like instrument) and ngombi (a stringed instrument) are used in various ceremonies and performances. Gabonese music and dance are vibrant expressions of cultural identity.

Cultural Festivals:
 Gabon's cultural calendar is marked by a variety of festivals that celebrate its diverse heritage. The "Ngondo" festival of the Fang people and the "Makina" festival of the Bapounou are examples of

events that showcase traditional dances, rituals, and communal gatherings.

Culinary Traditions:
 Gabonese cuisine reflects the country's cultural diversity. Staple foods include cassava, plantains, and rice. Dishes often feature a variety of sauces and ingredients, highlighting regional flavors and preferences.

Clothing and Attire:
 Traditional clothing varies among ethnic groups. For example, the Fang people are known for their distinctive woven fabrics and hairstyles, while other communities have their own clothing traditions, often characterized by vibrant colors and patterns.

Rites of Passage:
 Gabonese cultural diversity is expressed through various rites of passage, including birth ceremonies, initiation rituals, and funeral traditions. These events play a crucial role in maintaining cultural identity and transmitting values from one generation to the next.

Language and Oral Traditions:
 Oral traditions are vital in preserving cultural knowledge and stories. Griots, storytellers, and elders pass down history, folklore, and moral lessons through spoken word, ensuring the continuity of cultural heritage.

Contemporary Cultural Expression:
In addition to preserving traditional culture, Gabon
has a growing contemporary cultural scene.
Modern art, music genres like hip-hop and reggae,
and literature written by Gabonese authors
contribute to the evolving cultural landscape.

Global Influences:
Gabon's cultural diversity is not isolated but
interacts with global influences. The country's
openness to the world through trade, education,
and media has led to a dynamic blend of traditional
and contemporary elements.

Family and Social Structure:
Gabonese society places importance on family and
community bonds. Extended families often live
together or in close proximity, fostering strong
intergenerational relationships. Traditional social
structures, such as councils of elders, play a role in
decision-making and conflict resolution.

Rural and Urban Contrasts:
Gabon exhibits a contrast between rural and urban
lifestyles. While urban areas like Libreville have
experienced modernization and globalization, many
rural communities maintain traditional ways of life.
This dichotomy contributes to the country's cultural
diversity.

Gender Roles and Relationships:

Gender roles in Gabonese society are evolving. Traditionally, women played essential roles in family and community life, while men often held positions of authority. However, modernization and changing social norms are shifting gender dynamics.

Initiation and Coming-of-Age Rituals:
Coming-of-age rituals and initiation ceremonies are significant cultural practices. These rites mark the transition from childhood to adulthood and often involve tests of strength, endurance, and traditional teachings.

Traditional Medicine and Healing:
Traditional healing practices, such as herbal medicine and rituals conducted by traditional healers, are part of Gabon's cultural diversity. These practices coexist with modern healthcare and continue to be valued in some communities.

Cultural Symbols and Iconography:
Gabon is known for its intricate and symbolic art forms, including masks and sculptures. These artworks often feature representations of ancestors, spirits, and animals, carrying deep cultural and spiritual significance.

Storytelling and Oral Tradition:
Oral storytelling is a cherished tradition in Gabon. Elders and storytellers pass down myths, legends,

and historical narratives through verbal storytelling.
This preserves cultural memory and heritage.

Dress and Adornments:
 Traditional clothing and adornments vary by ethnic
group. Elaborate hairstyles, scarifications, and body
painting are among the ways Gabonese people
express their cultural identity through personal
adornment.

Marriage and Wedding Customs:
 Marriage customs vary among ethnic groups but
often involve ceremonies that reflect cultural beliefs
and values. These ceremonies may include
negotiations, dowries, and communal celebrations.

Cultural Change and Preservation:
 Gabon's cultural diversity faces challenges from
modernization, urbanization, and globalization.
Efforts to preserve traditional practices, language,
and rituals are essential for maintaining cultural
richness.

Youth and Cultural Revival:
 Younger generations in Gabon are increasingly
interested in preserving and revitalizing their
cultural heritage. Cultural festivals, art exhibitions,
and educational programs promote cultural
awareness among the youth.

Globalization and Fusion:

Global influences, including music, fashion, and technology, have impacted Gabonese culture. The fusion of traditional and contemporary elements creates a dynamic cultural landscape that continues to evolve.

Diaspora Communities:
Gabonese culture is also expressed through diaspora communities in other countries. Gabonese expatriates often maintain connections to their homeland by celebrating cultural events and traditions abroad.

In summary, Gabon's cultural diversity is a vibrant mosaic of ethnicities, languages, traditions, and artistic expressions. This diversity contributes to the country's unique identity within the African continent and enriches its cultural heritage.

Gabon's cultural diversity is a complex and dynamic tapestry woven from a myriad of traditions, beliefs, and practices. It reflects the country's rich history, ethnic pluralism, and the ongoing evolution of its cultural identity.

6. **Challenges and Development**: Despite its resource wealth, Gabon faces challenges such as income inequality, lack of diversification beyond oil, and concerns about governance and corruption. These challenges have shaped the country's development trajectory and political discourse.

Economic Diversification:
 Gabon faces the challenge of diversifying its economy away from heavy reliance on oil exports. Economic diversification efforts aim to develop other sectors such as agriculture, mining, and tourism to reduce vulnerability to oil price fluctuations.

Infrastructure Development:
 While Gabon has made significant progress in infrastructure development, particularly in urban areas, there's a need for continued investment in transportation, energy, and telecommunications infrastructure to support economic growth and regional connectivity.

Corruption and Governance:
 Corruption remains a challenge in Gabon, affecting various sectors including government, business, and public services. Ensuring good governance, transparency, and accountability is essential for sustainable development.

Youth Unemployment:
 Youth unemployment and underemployment are pressing issues. Addressing this challenge requires strategies for skills development, job creation, and entrepreneurship opportunities for young people.

Education and Skills Gap:

Despite improvements in the education sector, there's a need to bridge the skills gap to meet the demands of a diversified economy. Enhancing access to quality education and vocational training is crucial.

Healthcare Access:
Access to quality healthcare services, particularly in rural areas, remains a challenge. Strengthening healthcare infrastructure and addressing health disparities are priorities for improving the well-being of Gabonese citizens.

Environmental Conservation:
Balancing economic development with environmental conservation is a continuous challenge. Gabon's rich biodiversity requires robust conservation efforts to protect its unique ecosystems while promoting sustainable resource use.

Income Inequality:
Income inequality is a concern, with disparities between urban and rural areas and among different socioeconomic groups. Inclusive economic policies and social programs are necessary to reduce inequality.

Human Rights and Political Freedoms:
Ensuring the protection of human rights and political freedoms while maintaining political

stability is an ongoing challenge. Balancing these aspects is essential for democratic development.

Regional Security and Conflict Prevention:
 Gabon is situated in a region with complex security challenges, including threats from armed groups and transnational criminal activities. Strengthening regional security cooperation and conflict prevention efforts is important for stability.

Global Economic Trends:
 Global economic trends and shifts in demand for commodities, including oil, can impact Gabon's economic prospects. The country must adapt to changes in the global economy and explore opportunities in emerging sectors.

Climate Change Resilience:
 Climate change poses risks, including extreme weather events and rising sea levels. Building resilience and implementing climate adaptation measures are critical for Gabon's long-term development.

Foreign Investment and Partnerships:
 Attracting foreign investment and strengthening international partnerships for sustainable development is a priority. Gabon must strike a balance between fostering economic growth and protecting its national interests.

COVID-19 Pandemic Response:

The COVID-19 pandemic has posed health, economic, and social challenges. Managing the pandemic, ensuring vaccine access, and mitigating its impact on the economy are immediate concerns.

.

Electricity Access:
Improving electricity access in rural and remote areas remains a challenge. Expanding energy infrastructure and increasing access to electricity is essential for economic development and quality of life.

Digital Divide:
There is a digital divide in Gabon, with disparities in internet access and digital literacy, particularly in rural areas. Bridging this gap is vital for promoting education, e-commerce, and digital innovation.

Tourism Potential:
While Gabon has significant tourism potential due to its biodiversity and natural beauty, it faces challenges in developing sustainable tourism infrastructure and attracting visitors. Balancing tourism growth with conservation is crucial.

Food Security:
Ensuring food security, especially in rural communities, is essential. Promoting agricultural practices, improving irrigation, and addressing

issues like land tenure can enhance food production and reduce dependence on imports.

Healthcare Infrastructure:
Investment in healthcare infrastructure is needed to provide accessible and quality healthcare services to all Gabonese citizens. This includes expanding healthcare facilities, improving medical equipment, and increasing healthcare workforce capacity.

Youth Empowerment:
Empowering the youth through education, skills development, and job opportunities is a priority. Engaging young people in decision-making processes and providing avenues for entrepreneurship can contribute to national development.

Environmental Conservation and Sustainable Logging:
Balancing economic activities like logging with environmental conservation is a challenge. Promoting sustainable logging practices, enforcing regulations, and protecting critical ecosystems are ongoing efforts.

Land Rights and Resource Management:
Clear land tenure and resource management policies are essential for preventing conflicts over land and resources. Ensuring that local

communities benefit from resource extraction activities is crucial for sustainable development.

Climate Resilience and Disaster Preparedness:
 Gabon is vulnerable to climate change impacts, including extreme weather events. Strengthening climate resilience and disaster preparedness is vital for safeguarding lives and livelihoods.

Private Sector Growth:
 Fostering private sector growth and entrepreneurship is necessary for economic diversification. Creating a conducive business environment, reducing bureaucratic hurdles, and providing access to financing can stimulate private sector development.

Education Quality:
 While access to education has improved, ensuring the quality of education remains a challenge. Upgrading curriculum standards, training teachers, and enhancing educational infrastructure are steps toward improving education outcomes.

Social Safety Nets:
 Developing effective social safety nets and welfare programs is important for mitigating poverty and inequality. Such programs can provide a safety net for vulnerable populations during economic challenges.

Responsible Natural Resource Management:

Managing natural resources, including oil, timber, and minerals, responsibly is crucial for long-term sustainability. Gabon must ensure that resource extraction benefits both the economy and local communities.

Transparency and Corruption:
Addressing corruption and improving transparency in government operations and business transactions is vital for attracting foreign investment, enhancing governance, and fostering economic development.

In summary, Gabon faces a range of challenges as it seeks to achieve sustainable development. Addressing these challenges requires a combination of sound governance, investment in infrastructure and human capital, environmental stewardship, and adaptation to global economic dynamics. Gabon's development efforts are a complex journey that involves balancing these challenges with the country's unique opportunities and strengths

7. **Strategic Location**: Gabon's location along the Atlantic coast has given it strategic importance as a port and transportation hub for the Central African region.

Geographical Position:
Gabon is strategically located in Central Africa, along the Atlantic Ocean. It is situated on the west

coast of the African continent, bordering Equatorial Guinea, Cameroon, the Republic of the Congo, and the Atlantic Ocean.

Maritime Access:
Gabon's coastline along the Atlantic Ocean provides it with direct access to international maritime trade routes. Its ports, including Port-Gentil and Owendo, serve as vital gateways for shipping goods to and from Central Africa and beyond.

Economic Gateway:
Gabon's geographic location makes it a natural economic gateway to the landlocked Central African region. It serves as a transit point for the import and export of goods to neighboring countries, contributing to its role as a regional trade hub.

Resource-Rich Interior:
Gabon's proximity to resource-rich countries in Central Africa positions it as a hub for resource extraction and trade. It plays a significant role in the transportation of minerals, oil, timber, and other natural resources from the interior to global markets.

Transportation Infrastructure:
Gabon has invested in transportation infrastructure, including road networks and railways, that connect it to neighboring countries. This infrastructure

enhances its position as a transit and logistical hub for the region.

Regional Stability and Diplomacy:
Gabon's relative political stability has allowed it to engage in regional diplomacy and peacekeeping efforts. Its strategic location has enabled it to play a constructive role in regional security and stability, contributing to its reputation as a responsible actor in Central Africa.

Diverse Trade Partners:
Gabon's location at the crossroads of Central Africa has attracted diverse trade partners from Europe, Asia, and the Americas. These trade relationships have contributed to economic growth and global connectivity.

Tourism Potential:
Gabon's position along the Atlantic Ocean, with pristine beaches, rainforests, and unique biodiversity, makes it an attractive destination for eco-tourism. Its strategic location offers opportunities to tap into the growing tourism market.

Global Energy Dynamics:
As a significant oil producer, Gabon's strategic location impacts global energy dynamics. Its oil exports contribute to international energy markets and influence global oil prices.

Challenges and Opportunities:
While Gabon's strategic location offers numerous opportunities for trade, investment, and regional influence, it also presents challenges related to infrastructure development, regional conflicts, and competition with neighboring countries. Careful management of these factors is essential for maximizing its strategic advantages.

Geographical Position:
Gabon is strategically situated on the west coast of Central Africa, along the Gulf of Guinea. Its geographic location offers several advantages:

  Maritime Access: Gabon has access to the Atlantic Ocean, providing opportunities for international trade and shipping routes. Its ports, such as Port-Gentil and Owendo, serve as gateways for maritime commerce with both African and global partners.

  Proximity to Key Markets: Gabon's location places it in proximity to   regional markets in Central and West Africa, including countries like Cameroon, Equatorial Guinea, Republic of the Congo, and Nigeria. This geographical advantage facilitates trade and economic cooperation within the Central African region.

Transport Corridor: Gabon's road networks, combined with its neighboring countries, form an essential transport corridor connecting Central Africa to the Atlantic coast. This corridor enhances transportation of goods and people,

In summary, Gabon's strategic location along the Atlantic coast of Central Africa positions it as a vital player in regional trade, resource extraction, and diplomatic efforts. Its geographical advantages offer opportunities for economic development, while its stability and infrastructure investments contribute to its regional influence.

8. **Conservation Efforts**: Gabon has gained attention for its commitment to environmental conservation. Its dedication to protecting its rainforests and wildlife has earned it recognition in global conservation circles.

Biodiversity Protection:
Gabon is renowned for its extraordinary biodiversity, including pristine rainforests and a wide range of wildlife. Conservation efforts are focused on protecting these unique ecosystems and the numerous endangered species they harbor, such as forest elephants, gorillas, and pangolins.

National Parks and Reserves:
Gabon has established a network of national parks and wildlife reserves that cover a significant portion

of its territory. These protected areas, including Loango National Park and Ivindo National Park, serve as refuges for wildlife and are essential for biodiversity conservation.

Marine Conservation:
In addition to terrestrial conservation, Gabon has made significant strides in marine conservation. The establishment of marine protected areas, such as the Pongara National Park and the Mayumba National Park, helps safeguard coastal ecosystems and marine life.

Anti-Poaching Measures:
Combatting poaching is a top priority in Gabon. Anti-poaching units and ranger patrols are deployed to protect wildlife from illegal hunting and the illegal wildlife trade. Efforts to strengthen law enforcement and penalties for poaching are ongoing.

Community Engagement:
Engaging local communities in conservation efforts is vital for success. Collaborative programs involve communities in wildlife monitoring, sustainable resource management, and eco-tourism initiatives, helping to reduce human-wildlife conflicts and create economic opportunities.

Research and Data Collection:
Gabon hosts numerous research projects and collaborations with international organizations

aimed at studying biodiversity and ecosystems. Scientific research provides valuable data for conservation planning and management.

Eco-Tourism Development:
Gabon is exploring eco-tourism as a sustainable means of generating revenue while preserving natural habitats. Tourist facilities and infrastructure in and around national parks are being developed to provide visitors with opportunities to experience Gabon's natural beauty.

Sustainable Logging Practices:
Gabon recognizes the importance of sustainable forestry practices. Regulations are in place to ensure responsible logging and the protection of forest ecosystems. Gabon is working to balance economic interests with conservation needs.

International Partnerships:
Gabon collaborates with international organizations and conservation groups, such as the World Wildlife Fund (WWF) and the Wildlife Conservation Society (WCS), to support its conservation initiatives. These partnerships bring expertise and resources to conservation efforts.

Climate Change Mitigation:
Protecting Gabon's forests not only conserves biodiversity but also contributes to global climate change mitigation. Gabon has made commitments

to reduce deforestation and promote sustainable forest management as part of its climate action.

Challenges:
Gabon faces challenges in conservation efforts, including the encroachment of illegal logging, wildlife trafficking, and human-wildlife conflicts. Additionally, balancing conservation goals with economic development remains a complex task.

Eco-Guardianship:
Gabon is often referred to as an "eco-guardian" due to its commitment to preserving its natural treasures. The government's strong stance on conservation is evidenced by policies and actions aimed at protecting wildlife and ecosystems.

Low-Impact Tourism:
Gabon is promoting low-impact and sustainable tourism practices within its national parks and protected areas. Eco-friendly tourism initiatives ensure that visitors can experience the country's natural beauty while minimizing environmental impact.

Mangrove Conservation:
Mangroves play a vital role in coastal ecosystems and climate change mitigation. Gabon is actively engaged in mangrove conservation efforts, safeguarding these unique and fragile habitats.

Wildlife Research and Monitoring:
Continual research and monitoring of wildlife populations help Gabonese authorities make informed decisions about conservation. Collaboration with international researchers and organizations contributes to a deeper understanding of Gabon's biodiversity.

Transboundary Conservation:
Gabon collaborates with neighboring countries on transboundary conservation projects. Protecting shared ecosystems and corridors for wildlife is crucial for the long-term survival of species.

Education and Awareness:
Education and public awareness campaigns are essential components of Gabon's conservation strategy. Efforts to educate local communities, schools, and the public about the importance of preserving the environment contribute to conservation goals.

Conservation Legislation:
Gabon has enacted strict conservation laws and regulations to combat illegal wildlife trafficking and habitat destruction. Penalties for wildlife-related crimes are enforced to deter poaching and smuggling.

Community-Based Conservation:
Incorporating local communities into conservation initiatives not only benefits wildlife but also provides

economic opportunities for residents through sustainable resource management and eco-tourism activities.

Ranger Training and Capacity Building:
Empowering rangers and conservation professionals with training and resources enhances their ability to protect wildlife and natural habitats effectively.

International Collaboration:
Gabon actively engages in international forums and conventions related to conservation, such as the Convention on Biological Diversity (CBD) and the Ramsar Convention on Wetlands. These collaborations strengthen its commitment to global conservation efforts.

Sustainable Fishing Practices:
Gabon is working to promote sustainable fishing practices along its coastline, aiming to balance economic needs with the conservation of marine resources.

Eco-Friendly Infrastructure:
As Gabon develops infrastructure, there's an emphasis on minimizing environmental impact. Projects take into account the need to protect ecosystems and maintain ecological integrity.

Conservation Funding:

Gabon has sought funding from international donors and organizations to support its conservation efforts. Financial support is essential for the successful implementation of conservation programs.

In summary, Gabon is making significant strides in conservation efforts to protect its unique biodiversity, both on land and in its marine environments. These efforts involve a combination of protected areas, community engagement, research, and sustainable practices, positioning Gabon as a leader in African conservation.

Gabon's conservation efforts are multifaceted and holistic, encompassing terrestrial and marine ecosystems, community engagement, research, and sustainable practices. The country's dedication to eco-guardianship positions it as a leader in biodiversity conservation in Africa, contributing to the protection of its unique natural heritage.

9. **Literary and Cultural Contributions**: Gabon has a history of producing notable literary figures and artists who contribute to African literature and culture. Its unique cultural expressions have enriched the broader African cultural landscape.

Oral Tradition:
Gabon has a rich oral tradition that includes folktales, legends, and historical narratives passed down through generations. Griots and storytellers

play a vital role in preserving and transmitting this cultural heritage.

Literary Figures:
Gabon has produced notable literary figures who have contributed to African literature. Writers like René Philombé, Jean-Aimé Mouketou, and Justine Mintsa have produced works that explore Gabonese identity, history, and social issues.

Oral Poetry:
Oral poetry is a vibrant part of Gabonese culture. Poets recite and perform traditional poems that celebrate cultural values, historical events, and social themes. These poems often serve as vehicles for storytelling and moral lessons.

Bilingual Literature:
Many Gabonese writers produce works in both French (the official language) and Gabonese languages, creating a bridge between traditional oral forms of communication and contemporary literary expression.

Cultural Festivals:
Gabon hosts cultural festivals that celebrate its diverse ethnic traditions, music, dance, and art. Festivals like the Ngondo Festival and Makina Festival provide platforms for cultural exchange and preservation.

Contemporary Music and Art:

Gabonese musicians and artists contribute to the country's cultural vibrancy. Musicians like Patience Dabany and artists like Owanto have gained recognition both nationally and internationally, blending traditional influences with contemporary expressions.

Traditional Music and Dance:
Traditional music and dance are integral to Gabonese culture. Diverse ethnic groups have their own distinctive musical styles and dance forms, which are showcased during celebrations, ceremonies, and festivals.

Cultural Institutions:
Gabon has cultural institutions, such as the Gabonese National Museum, which house artifacts, art collections, and historical exhibitions that highlight the country's cultural heritage.

Promotion of Gabonese Literature:
The government and cultural organizations in Gabon actively promote Gabonese literature through literary events, book fairs, and writing competitions. These initiatives encourage literary creativity and the sharing of Gabonese stories.

Cultural Exchange Programs:
Gabon participates in international cultural exchange programs, fostering collaboration with artists, writers, and cultural institutions from around

the world. This exchange enriches Gabon's cultural landscape and promotes its heritage globally.

Language Preservation:
Efforts are underway to preserve and promote Gabonese languages through education and cultural programs. Language preservation is seen as a crucial aspect of maintaining cultural identity.

Historical Narratives:
Gabonese literature often delves into historical narratives, shedding light on the country's past, including its pre-colonial history, colonial experience, and post-independence era.

Film and Theater:
Gabon has a growing film and theater scene. Filmmakers and playwrights explore contemporary social issues and cultural themes through their work, contributing to the country's cultural discourse.

Cultural Diplomacy:
Gabon uses cultural diplomacy as a means to strengthen international ties and showcase its cultural richness. Cultural exchange programs, art exhibitions, and participation in global cultural events help promote Gabonese culture on the world stage.

Film Industry:

The Gabonese film industry is emerging, with filmmakers like Imunga Ivanga gaining recognition for their work. Movies such as "From a Whisper to a Roar" (D'un murmure à un cri) explore societal issues and contribute to cinematic diversity.

Folklore and Mythology:
Gabon's folklore and mythology are a source of inspiration for literature and the arts. These stories often contain valuable lessons and insights into the cultural and spiritual beliefs of Gabonese communities.

Architectural Heritage:
Gabon's architectural heritage includes traditional structures like Fang huts and Punu huts, which are characterized by their unique designs and construction techniques. These architectural styles reflect the cultural diversity of the country.

Fashion and Textiles:
Gabonese fashion designers draw from traditional patterns and textiles to create contemporary clothing that celebrates cultural identity. These designs often incorporate traditional motifs and colors.

Language Promotion:
Efforts to promote Gabonese languages include language preservation initiatives, literature written in local languages, and language education

programs. This helps maintain linguistic diversity and cultural heritage.

Culinary Arts:
Gabonese cuisine is diverse, featuring a range of dishes influenced by various ethnic groups. Staples like manioc, plantains, and palm nuts are used to create flavorful and unique dishes that contribute to Gabon's culinary identity.

Cultural Collaboration:
Gabon collaborates with neighboring countries in Central Africa to promote regional cultural integration. These collaborations foster cultural exchange, artistic synergy, and mutual understanding.

Art Galleries and Exhibitions:
Art galleries and exhibitions in Gabon provide a platform for both emerging and established artists to showcase their work. These spaces contribute to the growth of contemporary Gabonese art.

Cultural Preservation in Education:
Cultural education is integrated into Gabonese schools, ensuring that young generations learn about their heritage, traditional values, and the importance of cultural preservation.

Museums and Heritage Sites:
Gabon boasts museums and heritage sites that preserve and showcase the country's cultural and

historical artifacts. These institutions serve as repositories of Gabon's heritage for present and future generations.

Global Cultural Influence:
Gabonese artists, musicians, and writers have gained recognition on the international stage, contributing to the global appreciation of African culture and creativity.

Cross-Cultural Collaborations:
Collaborative projects between Gabonese artists and international counterparts foster cross-cultural exchanges and artistic innovation.

In summary, Gabon's cultural contributions extend beyond literature to encompass a wide range of artistic expressions, architectural heritage, culinary traditions, and cultural preservation efforts. These contributions are integral to Gabon's identity and its engagement with the global cultural community.

Gabon's significance lies in its biodiversity, oil production, diplomatic role, political stability, cultural diversity, and conservation efforts. While facing challenges, the country's history, geography, and contributions make it an important player in both regional and global contexts.

- Overview of political history

Pre-Colonial Period:

Before European colonization, Gabon was inhabited by various ethnic groups, each with its own political and social structures. The region had a history of trade and interaction with Arab and European traders along the coast.

The pre-colonial period in Gabon, like in many parts of Africa, is characterized by a rich and diverse history of indigenous cultures and societies. Here are some key details about Gabon's pre-colonial period:

1. Ethnic Diversity: Gabon was inhabited by a variety of Bantu-speaking ethnic groups, each with its own distinct culture, language, and traditions. Some of the prominent ethnic groups in Gabon include the Fang, Bapounou, Myene, and Baka, among others.

2. Social Structures: Pre-colonial Gabonese societies were organized into different social structures. Many of them had chieftaincies or kingdoms, with chiefs or kings at the helm. These

leaders often held spiritual and political authority within their communities.

3. Religion and Beliefs: Traditional African religions were prevalent, characterized by animism and the belief in spirits and ancestors. Religious practices and rituals played a central role in the lives of the people, guiding various aspects of their society, including governance and healthcare.

4. Trade and Commerce: Trade networks existed, both within Gabon and with neighboring regions. Valuable goods such as ivory, tropical hardwoods, and other forest products were traded. The Gabonese coast along the Atlantic Ocean also facilitated trade with European traders before formal colonization.

5. Art and Culture: Gabonese societies were known for their artistic achievements. They created intricate wooden sculptures, masks, and other art forms that were not only aesthetically significant but also held cultural and spiritual importance.

6. Subsistence Agriculture: Agriculture was a fundamental part of the pre-colonial economy. Communities practiced subsistence farming, growing crops like yams, plantains, cassava, and various vegetables. Hunting, fishing, and gathering were also important for sustenance.

7. Social Organization: Gabonese societies had well-defined social hierarchies, often based on age and gender. Elders held positions of respect and authority, and the roles and responsibilities of men and women in society were clearly defined.

8. Interactions with Neighbors: Gabon's geographical location meant that it had interactions and exchanges with neighboring regions, including Central Africa and West Africa. These interactions influenced aspects of culture, trade, and language.

9. Oral Tradition: Much of Gabon's pre-colonial history and knowledge was transmitted through oral tradition. Storytelling, songs, and proverbs were used to pass down cultural heritage and historical events.

10. Political Systems: While Gabon was home to various ethnic groups, each had its own political systems. Some societies were organized into centralized kingdoms ruled by kings or chiefs, while others had more decentralized systems with village councils and elders making communal decisions.

11. Trade Routes: Gabon's location allowed it to be part of important trade routes. For instance, the Ogowe River served as a natural highway for trade, connecting inland regions to the coast and facilitating commerce.

12. Ironworking: Many Gabonese communities engaged in ironworking, producing tools, weapons, and other metal goods. Iron smelting and blacksmithing were crucial skills passed down through generations.

13. Gender Roles: Gender roles in pre-colonial Gabon varied among different groups. In some societies, women held positions of power and influence, while in others, gender roles were more rigidly defined.

14. Military Organizations: Some Gabonese societies had well-organized military structures to defend against external threats and maintain internal order. Warriors played significant roles in these communities.

15. Religious Practices: Traditional religions were deeply ingrained in daily life. Worship of ancestral spirits and natural elements was common, and religious leaders held important roles in conducting ceremonies and rituals.

16. Oral History: The preservation of history and knowledge relied on oral traditions. Griots, or oral historians, were responsible for memorizing and passing down the history, genealogy, and legends of their communities.

17. Linguistic Diversity: Gabon is known for its linguistic diversity, with numerous Bantu languages

spoken across the country. Each ethnic group typically had its own language or dialect.

18. Artistic Expression: Gabonese art was highly diverse and expressive. Masks, sculptures, and textiles were adorned with intricate designs and patterns, often reflecting spiritual and cultural themes.

19. Kinship and Clan Structures: Kinship and clan systems were essential for social cohesion. People traced their lineage through these structures, which played a role in determining inheritance, marriage, and societal roles.

20. Conflict and Alliances: Interactions between different ethnic groups in Gabon were marked by both cooperation and conflict. Sometimes, alliances were formed for trade or defense against common adversaries.

It's important to note that the specifics of pre-colonial Gabonese history varied among different ethnic groups and regions. Additionally, the arrival of European colonial powers, particularly the French, significantly impacted and transformed Gabonese society and its trajectory.

Understanding Gabon's pre-colonial history provides valuable insights into the cultural richness and diversity of the region before external influences and colonialism reshaped its society and institutions.

Colonial Era:

In the late 19th century, Gabon became a French colony. It was part of French Equatorial Africa, which included several Central African territories. During this period, Gabon experienced European influence and the imposition of colonial administration.

Independence and Early Post-Colonial Years: Gabon gained independence from France on August 17, 1960, under the leadership of President Léon M'ba. In the early post-independence years, Gabon adopted a one-party system, with M'ba as the sole ruler.

During the colonial era, Gabon was under the rule of European colonial powers, primarily France. Here are details about Gabon's colonial period:

1. French Colonialism: Gabon came under French colonial control during the late 19th century as part of French Equatorial Africa. The French established control through treaties, military conquest, and diplomatic agreements.

2. Economic Exploitation: The primary motive for French colonization in Gabon was economic exploitation. Gabon was rich in resources such as

rubber, ivory, tropical hardwoods, and palm oil, which were extracted and exported to France.

3. Labor Practices: Forced labor was a common practice during the colonial era. Many Gabonese people were subjected to forced labor on plantations, in mining, and on public works projects. This labor system was often brutal and exploitative.

4. Administrative Structure: Gabon was incorporated into French Equatorial Africa, which had a centralized colonial administration. French officials were in charge of governing the colony, and French laws and customs were imposed.

5. Social and Cultural Impact: French colonialism had a profound impact on Gabonese society. Traditional customs and languages were often suppressed, and French culture and language were promoted. This led to a blending of cultures and the emergence of a creole culture known as "Gabonite."

6. Education and Religion: The French colonial government introduced formal education, but it was limited and mainly focused on training a small elite class. Christianity, particularly Catholicism, was promoted as the dominant religion.

7. Resistance and Rebellions: Gabonese people resisted colonial rule through various means, including protests and uprisings. The most

significant rebellion was the Kongo-Wara War (1928-1931), which saw widespread resistance against forced labor and taxation.

8. World War II: During World War II, Gabon briefly came under the control of the Vichy French government, which was aligned with Nazi Germany. In 1940, Free French forces, led by Charles de Gaulle, launched an operation to regain control of Gabon.

9. Post-War Changes: After World War II, there were increasing demands for greater autonomy and political representation. The French government introduced some reforms, including limited representation in the French National Assembly.

10. Path to Independence: Gabon's path to independence was relatively peaceful compared to some other African colonies. It gained full independence from France on August 16, 1960, with Léon M'ba as its first President.

11. Economic Dependence: Gabon's economy during the colonial period was heavily dependent on exports, particularly of rubber and timber. These industries were controlled by French companies, contributing to economic inequality.

12. Social Hierarchies: The French colonial administration often reinforced existing social hierarchies, including favoring certain ethnic groups

or elites over others. This had long-lasting social and political implications.

13. Impact on Traditional Institutions: Traditional political and social structures were often undermined by colonial rule. Traditional chiefs and leaders had their authority reduced or replaced by French-appointed officials.

14. Health and Healthcare: The colonial period saw the introduction of Western healthcare systems. While this brought some benefits, it also exposed Gabonese communities to new diseases. Access to healthcare was often limited, particularly in rural areas.

15. Land Ownership: Land ownership patterns changed during colonial rule. Much of the land was claimed by European settlers and companies, displacing local populations and disrupting traditional land tenure systems.

16. Migration and Urbanization: As a result of colonial economic policies, there was significant rural-to-urban migration. Cities like Libreville grew, leading to the emergence of urban centers and new social dynamics.

17. Cultural Preservation: Despite efforts to suppress traditional customs, many Gabonese communities managed to preserve elements of

their cultural heritage. Some traditional practices, dances, and ceremonies continued in secret.

18. African Soldiers in World Wars: Gabonese soldiers, known as "tirailleurs," fought in both World War I and World War II as part of French colonial forces. Their experiences in the wars contributed to a growing sense of political consciousness.

19. Education Disparities: Educational opportunities were limited for most Gabonese during the colonial era. The focus was primarily on providing education to a select few who were expected to serve the colonial administration.

20. Transition to Independence: Gabon's journey to independence was relatively smooth compared to some other African colonies, in part due to negotiations and political compromises. Léon M'ba, the first President, played a key role in this transition.

The colonial era left a lasting impact on Gabon, shaping its political, social, and economic landscape. The legacy of colonialism, including the influence of French language and culture, still plays a significant role in modern Gabonese society.

Gabon's colonial history left a complex legacy, with both positive and negative impacts. The struggle for independence and the post-colonial period marked a new chapter in Gabon's history, as the country sought to assert its sovereignty and address the legacies of colonialism.

Omar Bongo's Presidency:
After the death of M'ba in 1967, Omar Bongo became president and ruled for over four decades until his death in 2009. Bongo's presidency was characterized by stability, oil wealth, and efforts to diversify the economy.

Multiparty Democracy:
In 1990, amid political and social pressure, Gabon transitioned to a multiparty democracy. This led to the legalization of opposition parties and increased political pluralism.

2009 Presidential Election:
Omar Bongo's death in 2009 marked a historic transition. His son, Ali Bongo Ondimba, was elected as president in a disputed election. This election highlighted political tensions and concerns over the country's political future.

Political Stability and Challenges:
Ali Bongo's presidency was marked by efforts to modernize Gabon's economy and infrastructure. However, his rule faced criticism over allegations of electoral fraud and lack of transparency. Political protests and unrest occurred during his tenure.

2020 Presidential Election:

The 2020 presidential election was another pivotal moment in Gabonese politics. It resulted in a narrow victory for Ali Bongo, amid opposition claims of irregularities. The election highlighted ongoing political divisions.

Current Political Landscape:
As of my last knowledge update in September 2021, Gabon continues to navigate political challenges, including issues related to governance, transparency, and political opposition. Political stability remains a key concern.

Role in Regional Diplomacy:
Gabon has played a diplomatic role in regional affairs and peacekeeping efforts. It has been involved in regional organizations such as the African Union and the Economic Community of Central African States (ECCAS).

Economic Factors:
Gabon's political landscape is influenced by its significant oil wealth and efforts to diversify the economy. Economic stability and social development have been central to political discourse.

Constitutional Amendments:
During Ali Bongo's presidency, there were debates and changes to the constitution, which led to concerns about presidential term limits and the consolidation of power.

2021 Presidential Election:
In October 2021, Gabon held a presidential election
in which incumbent President Ali Bongo Ondimba
secured a victory, extending his presidency for
another term. The election was closely watched,
and the political landscape remained polarized.

Political Opposition and Protests:
The political opposition in Gabon has remained
active, with various parties and groups challenging
the ruling party's dominance. Protests and political
demonstrations have occurred, highlighting ongoing
political tensions.

Youth Engagement:
Youth activism and engagement in politics have
grown in significance. Younger generations are
increasingly vocal about their political aspirations
and concerns, contributing to the evolving political
landscape.

Efforts to Address Governance Challenges:
Gabon has made efforts to address governance
challenges, including corruption and transparency.
Anti-corruption measures and government reforms
have been initiated to improve accountability.

Regional and International Relations:
Gabon continues to be an active participant in
regional and international diplomacy. It plays a role

in regional organizations, peacekeeping missions, and environmental initiatives.

Economic Diversification:
Diversifying the economy away from heavy reliance on oil exports remains a priority. The government has implemented strategies to promote other sectors such as agriculture, mining, and tourism.

Infrastructure Development:
Gabon has invested in infrastructure projects, including transportation networks and energy production, to support economic growth and regional connectivity.

Environmental and Conservation Efforts:
Gabon maintains its commitment to environmental conservation, particularly the protection of its rainforests and wildlife. Initiatives to combat illegal logging and poaching continue.

COVID-19 Response:
Like many countries, Gabon faced challenges posed by the COVID-19 pandemic. The government implemented measures to mitigate the spread of the virus and address its impact on public health and the economy.

Presidential Term Limits:
Debates over presidential term limits and constitutional reforms have been a recurring topic

in Gabonese politics. The issue of political succession remains significant.

Press Freedom and Civil Liberties:
Press freedom and civil liberties have been subjects of discussion, with concerns raised about restrictions on media and civil society organizations.

Gabon's political history is characterized by a blend of stability, transitions, and political engagement. The country continues to navigate complex political dynamics, including efforts to address governance challenges, promote economic diversification, and strengthen democratic institutions. Political developments may have occurred since my last update, so it's advisable to consult recent sources for the latest information on Gabon's political landscape.

Regional Diplomacy: Gabon has played a role in mediating regional conflicts and fostering stability in Central Africa. Its participation in peacekeeping missions and efforts to resolve regional disputes contribute to its diplomatic influence.

Ethnic Diversity: Gabon is ethnically diverse, with numerous ethnic groups such as the Fang, Bantu, and Punu. The country's political landscape is influenced by ethnic considerations, and political alliances can be formed along ethnic lines.

Elections and Opposition: Elections in Gabon have often been contentious, with opposition parties accusing the ruling party of electoral irregularities. The political opposition continues to be a vocal force in the country's political discourse.

Human Rights: Human rights concerns have been raised in Gabon, particularly regarding issues related to freedom of speech and assembly. International human rights organizations have monitored the situation in the country.

Security Challenges: Gabon, like some other Central African nations, has faced security challenges, including threats from armed groups in the region. The government has taken measures to enhance national security.

Youth Engagement: Younger generations in Gabon are increasingly engaging in politics and civil society. Youth-led initiatives and activism contribute to the evolving political landscape.

Economic Policy: Economic policy has been a significant focus in Gabon's politics. The government has sought to balance economic development, diversification, and social welfare while managing the volatility of oil prices.

Constitutional Reforms: Debates over constitutional reforms, including changes to presidential term limits, have been a recurring theme in Gabonese politics. These discussions often spark political debates and protests.

Women in Politics: While women's representation in politics has been limited historically, there have been efforts to promote gender equality in political leadership, including through the adoption of gender quotas.

International Partnerships: Gabon maintains diplomatic relations with a range of countries and international organizations, furthering its role in regional and global affairs.

Gabon's political history and dynamics are shaped by a complex interplay of factors, including ethnic diversity, governance challenges, economic considerations, and regional diplomacy. The political situation in any country can evolve, so it's advisable to consult recent sources for the most up-to-date information on Gabon's politics and governance.

Chapter 2
Pre-Coup Gabon

- **Early political landscape**
- **Rise of the Bongo family**
- **Socioeconomic conditions**

- Early political landscape

The early political landscape of Gabon was characterized by the transition from a French colony to an independent nation. Here's an overview of the early political landscape:

Pre-Independence Political Movements:
Before gaining independence in 1960, Gabon did not have a long history of organized political movements for independence like some other African nations. Instead, the focus was on improving the social and economic conditions of the population within the colonial framework.

Independence Movement:

Gabon's path to independence was relatively peaceful. It achieved independence from France on August 17, 1960, under the leadership of President Léon M'ba. M'ba was the leader of the Gabon Democratic and Social Union (UDSG), which later became the Gabonese Democratic Party (PDG).

One-Party State:
After independence, Gabon adopted a one-party state system under M'ba's leadership. The PDG became the sole political party, and M'ba consolidated power. This one-party system lasted for several years.

Omar Bongo's Ascendancy:
Upon the death of President Léon M'ba in 1967, Omar Bongo Ondimba, who had served as vice president, took over as president. His long presidency would span over four decades, making him one of the longest-serving leaders in African history.

Political Stability and Oil Wealth:
Omar Bongo's presidency was characterized by political stability and economic growth, largely due to Gabon's significant oil reserves. Oil revenues fueled economic development and infrastructure projects.

Political Monopoly and Opposition:
During this period, the PDG continued to be the dominant political force, and opposition parties

faced challenges. The political landscape was marked by limited political pluralism.

Transition to Multiparty Democracy:
Amid growing political and social pressure, Gabon transitioned to a multiparty democracy in the early 1990s. Opposition parties were legalized, and Gabon held its first multiparty elections.

Political Evolution:
The political landscape evolved with the emergence of opposition parties and the holding of competitive elections. Gabonese politics became more pluralistic, although the PDG remained a significant political force.

Political Opposition and Elections:
Gabonese politics saw the rise of opposition figures and parties challenging the dominance of the PDG. Elections in the late 20th and early 21st centuries were often marked by political debates and competition.

Continued Political Evolution:
Gabon's political landscape continued to evolve, with presidential elections, legislative elections, and local elections being held at regular intervals.

.

Cold War Dynamics:
During the early years of independence, Gabon, like many African nations, was caught up in the Cold War politics. The country maintained diplomatic relations with both Western and Eastern bloc countries, trying to balance superpower interests.

Economic Development:
The early political landscape in Gabon included efforts to promote economic development and social progress. Oil wealth played a significant role in financing infrastructure projects, education, and healthcare initiatives.

Foreign Policy:
Gabon pursued a non-aligned foreign policy and played a role in regional and international diplomacy. It was involved in peacekeeping efforts and diplomatic negotiations in Central Africa.

Omar Bongo's Leadership:
Omar Bongo Ondimba's presidency, which began in the late 1960s, marked a period of continuity in Gabonese politics. His leadership style emphasized stability and economic growth.

Political Parties and Opposition:
The Gabonese Democratic Party (PDG), led by Omar Bongo, was the dominant political party during this era. Opposition parties, while present, faced challenges in gaining political influence.

Societal Changes:
Gabon experienced societal changes during this period, including urbanization and the expansion of education and healthcare services. These changes contributed to shifts in political awareness and aspirations.

Role of Traditional Authorities:
Traditional authorities, such as tribal chiefs and elders, continued to hold significance in Gabonese society. Their roles in local governance and decision-making were intertwined with modern political structures.

Press Freedom and Media:
The early political landscape saw some limitations on press freedom and media expression. The government exercised control over media outlets, which influenced the flow of information.

Pan-Africanism:
Gabon was influenced by the Pan-African movement, which advocated for African unity and solidarity. The country hosted international conferences and meetings related to Pan-Africanism.

International Aid and Development:
Gabon received development assistance from various countries and international organizations to

support its economic and social development initiatives.

Urbanization and Migration:
Gabon experienced urbanization as people migrated to cities in search of economic opportunities. Urban centers like Libreville grew in importance.

Educational Expansion:
Investments were made in education, with the aim of improving literacy rates and providing access to quality education for Gabonese citizens.

Healthcare Improvement:
Efforts were made to expand healthcare services and infrastructure, addressing health challenges in the country.

This early political landscape set the stage for the development of Gabon's political system and the interplay of political forces in the country. It marked the transition from a colonial territory to an independent nation with its own political institutions and dynamics. Political developments have continued since this early period, with a range of political parties and civil society organizations participating in the country's political discourse

- Rise of the Bongo family

The rise of the Bongo family to political prominence in Gabon is a significant aspect of the country's modern political history:

1. Omar Bongo Ondimba: The Bongo family's political ascent began with Omar Bongo Ondimba, who was born in 1935. He entered politics during the late colonial era and played a role in the transition to independence. In 1967, following the death of President Léon M'ba, Omar Bongo became President of Gabon.

2. Longevity in Office: Omar Bongo's presidency was marked by its longevity. He served as Gabon's President for over four decades, making him one of the longest-serving heads of state in African history. During his rule, Gabon experienced stability and economic growth, largely driven by oil revenues.

3. Political Dominance: Omar Bongo's Gabonese Democratic Party (PDG) was the dominant political force in Gabon. He maintained power through a combination of political maneuvering, control over state resources, and electoral victories that were often marred by allegations of fraud.

4. Economic Prosperity: Gabon's economy benefited from its oil wealth during Omar Bongo's

rule. However, despite the nation's significant oil revenues, there were concerns about wealth distribution and corruption.

5. Death and Succession: Omar Bongo passed away in 2009. His death marked a transition in Gabonese politics. His son, Ali Bongo Ondimba, succeeded him as President. This dynastic succession was met with mixed reactions, both domestically and internationally.

6. Ali Bongo's Presidency: Ali Bongo's presidency faced challenges and controversies. His rule was marked by efforts to diversify the economy and address social issues. However, allegations of electoral irregularities and political tensions persisted.

7. Political Opposition: Opposition parties in Gabon raised concerns about the legitimacy of Ali Bongo's presidency and contested election results. This led to periodic protests and political unrest.

8. Ongoing Influence: The Bongo family has continued to play a prominent role in Gabonese politics, with family members holding key government positions. This has raised questions about the consolidation of power within the family.

9. Evolving Political Landscape: Gabon's political landscape has been evolving, with increasing calls for political reforms, greater transparency, and

improved governance. The Bongo family's continued influence remains a topic of debate in Gabonese politics.

10. Bongo Family Network: The Bongo family established a powerful network within Gabonese politics and society. Family members held key positions in government, the military, and business, consolidating their influence.

11. Economic Ventures: The Bongo family's influence extended to various sectors of the economy, including ownership of businesses and access to lucrative contracts. This economic power further solidified their position in Gabonese society.

12. Foreign Relations: During Omar Bongo's presidency, Gabon maintained diplomatic ties with a range of countries and played a role in regional and international affairs. The Bongo family's relationships with foreign leaders, particularly in France, were instrumental in bolstering Gabon's standing on the global stage.

13. Criticism and Controversies: The Bongo family faced allegations of corruption, embezzlement of state funds, and human rights abuses during their rule. Such accusations led to scrutiny from international organizations and human rights advocates.

14. Political Transition Challenges: Ali Bongo's succession to the presidency was met with legal and political challenges. Opposition parties questioned the legitimacy of his victory in the 2009 election, resulting in protests and unrest.

15. Political Reforms: During Ali Bongo's presidency, there were discussions about political reforms and a national dialogue to address political tensions. However, progress on these fronts was slow, and some opposition leaders called for greater transparency and democratic changes.

16. Regional and Global Influence: Gabon, under the leadership of the Bongo family, continued to play a role in regional organizations such as the African Union and the Economic Community of Central African States (ECCAS). This allowed Gabon to assert itself as a diplomatic player in Central Africa.

17. Ali Bongo's Health Concerns: In 2018, Ali Bongo suffered a stroke while abroad, leading to questions about his fitness for office and a period of uncertainty in Gabonese politics.

18. Changing Political Landscape: Gabon's political landscape has evolved with the emergence of new political actors and parties. The Bongo family's influence has faced challenges from opposition forces advocating for democratic reforms.

It's important to note that my knowledge is based on information available up to September 2021, and the political situation in Gabon may have evolved since then. The Bongo family's influence in Gabon remains a significant topic in the country's politics and has been a subject of both domestic and international interest.

- Socioeconomic conditions

Overview

Gabon, a central African country, is rich in natural resources. Located on the Atlantic Ocean, it borders Cameroon, Equatorial Guinea, and the Republic of Congo. It is sparsely populated, with a population of 2.3 million (2021) and forests covering 88% of its territory.

Gabon has one of the highest urbanization rates in Africa with more than four in five Gabonese citizens live in cities. Libreville and Port-Gentil are home to 59% of the country's population. One in two Gabonese citizens is under the age of 20 and the fertility rate in urban areas is four children per woman against six in rural areas.

As a result of efforts to reduce emissions and preserve its vast rainforest, Gabon is a net carbon absorber and a leader in net zero emission initiatives. It has a rich ecosystem with extensive endowments of fertile land, coastal resources, and fisheries. However, despite its economic potential, the country is struggling to translate its resource wealth into sustainable and inclusive growth.

Political Context

The Gabonese Democratic Party (Parti démocratique gabonais, PDG) has dominated the political landscape for 55 years. President Ali Bongo Ondimba succeeded his father Omar Bongo Ondimba in 2009 and was re-elected in August 2016 in a highly controversial election marked by a low turnout (59%). Legislative and municipal elections held in 2018 saw a sweeping victory for the PDG, which retained its two-thirds majority in the National Assembly.

With less than six months before the end of the presidential term, Gabon is preparing for several milestones, the presidential and legislative and local elections, scheduled for 2023. A government reshuffle has taken place in January 2023, whereby President Ali Bongo Ondimba appointed a new Prime Minister.

Political consultations between the PDG and several opposition parties were held in February

2023, culminating in several agreements including on the following issues: (a) reintroduction of single-round ballot for all elections (replacing the two-round system), (b) a five-year term for the president, senators, deputies, and local elected officials (replacing seven-year and six-year terms), and (c) no reelection limitations for all political offices (previously elected officials were limited to two terms).

Economic Overview

Gabon, the fourth largest oil producer in Sub-Saharan Africa, posted strong economic growth over the past decade, driven mainly by oil and manganese production. In 2020, the oil sector accounted for 38.5% of GDP and 70.5% of exports despite efforts to diversify the economy.

Forecast at 3.4% before COVID-19, Gabon posted a -1.8% growth in 2020. The restrictive measures adopted to combat the pandemic and address the decline in oil prices in 2020 have resulted in rising unemployment and a sharp drop in domestic revenue mobilization, followed by a decline in exports and foreign direct investment, leading to a significant fiscal deficit.

Economic and social Outlook

Ukraine's invasion has impeded Gabon's economic growth. Gabonese households have been facing a rise in food price since the beginning of 2022 as the inflation rate reached 4.3% that same year. However, Gabon has taken steps to fight the high cost of living including temporally price caps for 48 imported consumer goods from October 2022 to March 2023. A new ministry devoted to the fight against the high cost of living was created in January 2023.

Gabon's economy is gradually recovering, supported by good performance in the oil, mining, and wood sectors. The removal of pandemic-related restrictions in March 2022 also contributed to growth in the services sector. GDP is estimated to be 3.1% in 2022, up from 1.5% in 2021. Moreover, the fiscal balance turned into a surplus of 3.0% of GDP in 2022 from a deficit of 1.9% in 2021.

Thanks to the gradual recovery, public debt declined in 2022, down to 52% of GDP against 60.7% in 2021. According to the July 2022 IMF Debt Sustainability Analysis, public debt is deemed sustainable, and risks have moderated

Development Challenges

Economic diversification, climate change and human capital building are priorities for the authorities, which are adopting series of measures to Promote green and resilient development and improve the business climate.

Faced with a 33%poverty rate, the government focuses its social policy on the following three pillars:

Establishing integrated social programs for the most vulnerable.
Creating income-generating activities for the poorest population groups; and
Reducing inequalities in access to basic public services.
In addition to delivering global public goods, forests provide opportunities for building local resilience and supporting economic diversification. The country has demonstrated a strong leadership to environmental protection through solid policy commitments. Gabon became the first country in Africa to receive results-based payments for reduced emissions from deforestation and forest degradation in 2021. It has hosted early March 2023, the One Forest Summit with France. The event sought a fair agreement between forest countries and the international community, to reconcile environmental ambition and economic development.

World Bank Group Engagement in Gabon

Gabon is eligible for the World Bank's IBRD (International Bank for Reconstruction and

Development) window for middle-income and creditworthy poor countries. On November 22, the World Bank Group's endorsed a new five-year Country Partnership Framework (CPF) for Gabon, which will cover fiscal years 2023 to 2027 to support the country's transition towards sustainable and inclusive economic growth. The new CPF will contribute to two higher-level outcomes, namely: (i) greater household resilience and (ii) increased employment in the non-oil private sector. The new framework also builds on Gabon's development strategy, the Transformation Acceleration Plan (PAT), and the World Bank's Regional Strategy.

This highly selective engagement targets the following areas:

A strong public service delivery system:
Gabon has made considerable progress on digital transformation
and broadband connectivity. To improve service delivery, the Bank will support digitization of key public services through the Digital Gabon project. The goal is to deliver more efficient and quality public services and improve public sector accountability and transparency.
Increased access to social services:
More investments are being made to boost access to electricity, water, and sanitation in underserved neighborhoods, and to expand social protection to the most vulnerable. It also involves well-designed

and targeted safety net systems to reduce unemployment and increase labor productivity.
Improved resilient urban infrastructure:
With one of the highest urbanization rates in Africa, Gabon needs to promote integrated urban development. This means better urban planning, improving roads and local transport, and greater access to greener and more resilient infrastructure in underserved neighborhoods.
Increased private investment in non-oil sectors:
To diversify the economy and improve the investment climate, the World Bank, together with IFC and the Multilateral Investment Guarantee Agency (MIGA), will promote blue and green jobs in key sectors such as fisheries, forestry and ecotourism. This will involve continued support to the Kinguele Aval hydro project and the upgrading of the Transgabonais railway.
The World Bank's active portfolio in Gabon comprises of 6 active projects outlined in the previous CPF for total commitments of $318.62 million in various development sectors including Energy and Extractives, Education, Poverty and Equity and Health.

Chapter 3

Factors Leading to the Coup

- **Discontentment and opposition**
- **Economic challenges**
- **Corruption and governance issues**

- Discontentment and opposition

Discontentment and opposition have been recurring themes in Gabonese politics, reflecting the complex dynamics of the country's political landscape.

1. Election Disputes: Electoral disputes have been a source of discontentment and opposition in Gabon. Opposition parties and candidates have, at times, alleged irregularities and fraud in presidential and legislative elections. These disputes have led to protests and challenges to the legitimacy of election outcomes.

2. Political Polarization: Gabon's political landscape is marked by polarization between the ruling party, traditionally the Gabonese Democratic Party (PDG), and various opposition groups. This polarization has sometimes resulted in confrontations and political tensions.

3. Civil Society Activism: Civil society organizations, including human rights groups and youth organizations, have played a significant role in expressing discontent and opposition to government policies. They advocate for greater transparency, accountability, and democratic reforms.

4. Youth Unrest: Gabon has a young population, and youth unemployment and disillusionment have fueled protests and social unrest. Young activists have been at the forefront of calling for political change and economic opportunities.

5. Protest Movements: Gabon has witnessed protest movements and demonstrations on various issues, including calls for political reforms, better economic conditions, and social justice. Protests have occasionally led to clashes with security forces.

6. Opposition Parties: Opposition parties have sought to challenge the dominance of the ruling party through electoral means and by mobilizing

popular support. These parties have diverse ideologies and constituencies.

7. Media Freedom: Freedom of the press and media independence have been contentious issues in Gabon. Journalists and media outlets have faced restrictions, and there have been incidents of harassment and censorship.

8. Calls for Constitutional Reforms: Calls for constitutional reforms, including changes to presidential term limits and the electoral system, have been central to opposition demands for a more inclusive political process.

9. Legal Challenges: Opposition figures have sometimes used legal channels, including the courts, to challenge election results and government actions. These legal battles have shaped the political discourse.

10. Regional Discontent: Discontentment and opposition are not limited to the capital, Libreville, but can also be found in various regions of Gabon. Local grievances and demands for equitable resource distribution have led to localized protests.

11. International Attention: Discontentment and opposition in Gabon have drawn international attention and concern. International observers and organizations have monitored elections and expressed support for democratic processes.

12. Dialogue and Reconciliation: At times, efforts at political dialogue and reconciliation have been initiated to address discontentment and opposition. These dialogues aim to find common ground and solutions to political challenges.

13. Economic Disparities: Economic inequality and disparities in wealth distribution have contributed to discontentment. Despite the country's oil wealth, there are significant income inequalities, with a portion of the population experiencing poverty and limited access to basic services.

14. Resource Management: Concerns about the management of Gabon's natural resources, particularly its oil wealth, have fueled opposition. There have been calls for greater transparency in the oil sector and the equitable distribution of oil revenues.

15. Human Rights Concerns: Human rights issues, including allegations of political repression, arbitrary arrests, and limitations on freedom of expression, have been raised by opposition groups and international organizations. These concerns have led to tensions and opposition to government actions.

16. Exiled Opposition Figures: Some opposition leaders and activists have gone into exile due to

political persecution or threats to their safety. Their exile has often been a form of opposition, as they continue to advocate for political change from abroad.

17. Youth Mobilization: Gabonese youth have increasingly mobilized through social media and online platforms to express discontent and organize protests. Social media has played a significant role in mobilizing and coordinating opposition activities.

18. International Relations: Gabon's foreign relations, particularly its alignment with certain foreign powers, have been a source of opposition criticism. Opposition groups have at times accused the government of favoring foreign interests over domestic ones.

19. Calls for Democratic Reforms: Opposition parties and civil society organizations have consistently called for democratic reforms aimed at enhancing political participation, electoral transparency, and good governance.

20. Local Governance: Discontentment at the local level has led to opposition to certain local government decisions, resource allocation, and land disputes. These local grievances can feed into broader political opposition.

21. Nonviolent Activism: While protests and demonstrations have occurred, there is also a

tradition of nonviolent activism in Gabon. Civil disobedience, advocacy campaigns, and other peaceful methods are used to express discontent and opposition.

22. International Support for Opposition: Opposition groups in Gabon have sought support from international partners, including neighboring countries and international organizations, to raise awareness of their grievances and seek mediation in political disputes.

23. Youth Political Participation: Youth engagement in politics goes beyond protest; some young Gabonese are actively involved in political parties, civil society organizations, and grassroots initiatives to advocate for change.

24. Diversity of Opposition: Gabon's opposition is not monolithic and includes a range of political ideologies, interests, and priorities. This diversity can influence the nature and strategies of opposition activities.

25. Role of Diaspora: Gabonese living in the diaspora have also played a role in opposition movements. They use their international networks to draw attention to political issues in Gabon and support opposition efforts.

Overall, discontentment and opposition in Gabon are multifaceted, encompassing a wide range of political, economic, social, and human rights concerns. These dynamics continue to shape the country's political landscape and influence the trajectory of Gabonese politics.

It's important to note that political dynamics can evolve over time, and the specific issues of discontentment and opposition may vary. Gabon continues to grapple with the complex task of managing political tensions while working towards national unity and development.

- Economic challenges

Gabon has faced various economic challenges over the years, despite its significant oil wealth:

1. Oil Dependency: One of Gabon's most significant economic challenges is its heavy reliance on oil exports. Oil revenues have historically accounted for a substantial portion of the country's income, making the economy vulnerable to fluctuations in global oil prices.

2. Economic Diversification: Gabon has struggled to diversify its economy away from oil dependency. Efforts to develop other sectors, such as agriculture, manufacturing, and tourism, have been hindered by a lack of infrastructure and investment.

3. Income Inequality: Despite its oil wealth, Gabon experiences income inequality, with a significant portion of the population living in poverty. The benefits of economic growth have not been evenly distributed.

4. Unemployment and Youth Discontent: High unemployment rates, particularly among the youth, have contributed to social discontent and protests. Many young Gabonese struggle to find job opportunities that match their skills and aspirations.

5. Fiscal Sustainability: Gabon's fiscal policies have at times faced challenges in maintaining sustainability. Managing government expenditures and ensuring a stable fiscal framework has been a concern.

6. Public Debt: Gabon's public debt levels have risen, partly due to infrastructure investments and social spending. Managing debt levels while sustaining economic growth has been a priority.

7. Infrastructure Development: Despite efforts to improve infrastructure, Gabon still faces challenges in providing adequate transportation, energy, and telecommunications networks, which can hinder economic development.

8. Private Sector Development: Promoting a vibrant private sector has been a challenge. Encouraging entrepreneurship, attracting foreign investment, and

reducing bureaucracy are key areas for improvement.

9. Currency Stability: Maintaining currency stabllity in a volatile economic environment has been a challenge. Gabon uses the Central African CFA franc, which is pegged to the euro, and external economic shocks can impact the exchange rate.

10. Corruption and Governance: Corruption and governance issues have occasionally hindered economic development and discouraged foreign investment. Efforts to improve transparency and reduce corruption are ongoing.

11. Global Economic Uncertainty: Gabon's economy is influenced by global economic conditions, and external factors such as changes in oil prices and global economic downturns can impact its economic stability.

12. Environmental Sustainability: While Gabon has a wealth of natural resources, including forests and minerals, there is a need to balance resource extraction with environmental sustainability and conservation efforts.

13. Access to Education and Skills Development: Ensuring access to quality education and skills development is crucial for preparing the workforce for a diversified economy. Addressing gaps in education and training is an ongoing challenge.

14. Regional Economic Integration: Gabon is part of regional economic blocs such as the Economic Community of Central African States (ECCAS) and the Central African Economic and Monetary Community (CEMAC). Strengthening regional economic cooperation and integration is a priority.

15. Foreign Exchange Reserves: Gabon's foreign exchange reserves have faced fluctuations due to its dependence on oil exports. Maintaining an adequate level of reserves to support the currency and imports is a concern during periods of low oil prices.

16. Social Services: Despite efforts to expand access to healthcare and education, there are challenges in providing quality social services to all citizens, especially in rural and remote areas.

17. Infrastructure Gaps: While there have been infrastructure development projects, there remain gaps in transportation networks, energy supply, and telecommunications infrastructure, which can hinder economic growth and access to markets.

18. Agricultural Potential: Gabon has significant agricultural potential, but the sector has not been fully tapped. Challenges include land tenure issues, lack of modern farming techniques, and limited access to markets for agricultural products.

19. Youth Unemployment: High youth unemployment rates have led to social unrest and discontentment. Addressing youth unemployment is a pressing challenge, especially given the country's youthful population.

20. Trade Imbalances: Gabon has faced trade imbalances due to its reliance on imports for many goods and services. Efforts to promote domestic production and reduce import dependency are ongoing.

21. Economic Shocks: The economy of Gabon is susceptible to external economic shocks, such as fluctuations in oil prices and global economic crises. Diversifying the economy is essential to reduce vulnerability to such shocks.

22. Access to Finance: Access to finance, particularly for small and medium-sized enterprises (SMEs), remains limited. Expanding access to credit and financial services for businesses is crucial for economic growth.

23. Sustainable Development: Balancing economic development with environmental sustainability and conservation of Gabon's rich biodiversity is a challenge. Efforts to promote sustainable and eco-friendly practices are important.

24. Investor Confidence: Maintaining investor confidence and attracting foreign investment

requires a stable and transparent business environment. Addressing governance and corruption issues is key to achieving this.

25. Global Competition: Gabon competes globally for foreign investment and trade opportunities. In a highly competitive global marketplace, the country faces the challenge of positioning itself as an attractive destination for business and trade.

26. Crisis Management: Preparing for and managing crises, such as the impact of the COVID-19 pandemic, requires effective policies and strategies to mitigate economic disruptions and protect public health.

27. Access to Technology: Bridging the digital divide and ensuring access to modern technology and the internet in all regions of the country is essential for economic development and competitiveness.

Gabon recognizes these economic challenges and has embarked on various initiatives and reforms to address them. These efforts include economic diversification, improving the business environment, investing in human capital, and promoting sustainable development practices. Nonetheless, addressing these challenges remains a complex and ongoing process.

Efforts to address these economic challenges in Gabon involve implementing economic reforms, promoting private sector growth, improving infrastructure, and diversifying the economy. Additionally, pursuing sustainable development and addressing social inequalities are essential components of Gabon's economic agenda.

- Corruption and governance issues

Corruption and governance issues have been significant challenges in Gabon, affecting various aspects of the country's political and economic landscape. Here's a closer look at these issues:

Corruption:

1. Transparency International Rankings: Gabon has often ranked poorly on Transparency International's Corruption Perceptions Index, indicating that corruption is perceived as a significant issue within the country.

2. Bribery and Embezzlement: Corruption in Gabon includes various forms, such as bribery, embezzlement of public funds, and kickbacks. These corrupt practices can undermine public trust and divert resources from essential services.

3. Corruption in Public Procurement: Corrupt practices in public procurement have been a

concern. This can lead to inflated costs for public projects and reduce the quality of services delivered.

4. Natural Resource Sector: The oil sector, a crucial part of Gabon's economy, has faced allegations of corruption. Ensuring transparency and accountability in the management of oil revenues has been challenging.

5. Land and Resource Allocation: Corruption in land allocation and resource management can result in unfair distribution of resources and hinder economic development.

6. Customs and Tax Evasion: Customs and tax evasion are areas where corruption has been identified, leading to revenue losses for the government.

Governance Issues:
7. Political Dominance: The dominance of a single political party, historically the Gabonese Democratic Party (PDG), has raised concerns about political pluralism and competitive elections.

8. Limited Political Competition: Opposition parties have sometimes faced obstacles in participating effectively in elections, including allegations of electoral irregularities.

9. Rule of Law: Ensuring the rule of law and an independent judiciary has been a challenge. Political interference in the judicial system can undermine its impartiality.

10. Media Freedom: Freedom of the press and media independence have faced restrictions in Gabon. Journalists have at times been subject to harassment and censorship.

11. Civil Society Space: Civil society organizations and activists have occasionally faced limitations on their activities and the space for civic engagement.

12. Human Rights Concerns: Concerns about human rights issues, including arbitrary arrests and limitations on freedom of expression and assembly, have been raised by both domestic and international organizations.

Efforts to Address Corruption and Governance Issues:

13. Anti-Corruption Initiatives: Gabon has initiated anti-corruption measures, including the establishment of the National Agency for the Fight against Corruption (ANLC). These efforts aim to enhance transparency and accountability.

14. Constitutional Reforms: Debates over constitutional reforms, including changes to presidential term limits, have been part of the

governance discourse. These discussions can impact the country's political landscape.

15. Civil Society and Media: Civil society organizations and media outlets have played a role in raising awareness about corruption and governance issues, pushing for reforms and greater transparency.

16. International Engagement: Gabon has engaged with international organizations and partners to address corruption and improve governance. These collaborations can provide technical assistance and support for reforms.

17. Election Monitoring: International election observers have been invited to monitor Gabon's elections, contributing to efforts to ensure fair and transparent electoral processes.

18. Whistleblower Protection: Providing legal protection and support for whistleblowers who report corruption is an important aspect of anti-corruption efforts. Encouraging individuals to come forward with information can help uncover corrupt practices.

19. Asset Recovery: Gabon has made efforts to recover assets obtained through corrupt practices. Asset recovery initiatives aim to return misappropriated funds to the state and deter future corruption.

20. Public Financial Management: Improving public financial management and budgetary transparency is essential to prevent corruption in the allocation and use of public funds.

21. International Anti-Corruption Agreements: Gabon is a signatory to international anti-corruption agreements, such as the United Nations Convention against Corruption (UNCAC). Implementing the provisions of these agreements can strengthen anti-corruption measures.

22. Capacity Building: Building the capacity of government institutions, law enforcement agencies, and the judiciary to investigate and prosecute corruption cases is vital for effective anti-corruption efforts.

23. Civil Society Engagement: Civil society organizations, including anti-corruption groups, play a critical role in advocating for transparency and accountability. They monitor government actions and raise awareness about corruption issues.

24. Access to Information: Ensuring access to government information, including budgetary data and procurement details, is crucial for transparency. Access to information laws can facilitate this.

25. Ethics and Code of Conduct: Promoting ethical behavior and enforcing codes of conduct for public officials can help create a culture of integrity within government institutions.

26. Political Will: The commitment of political leaders to combat corruption is essential. Demonstrating political will to address corruption issues is a key driver of reform efforts.

27. Judicial Independence: Ensuring the independence of the judiciary is vital for holding individuals involved in corrupt practices accountable. A judiciary that is free from political interference is better equipped to adjudicate corruption cases.

28. International Partnerships: Collaboration with international partners, including organizations like the World Bank and the International Monetary Fund, can provide technical expertise and financial support for governance and anti-corruption programs.

29. Youth Engagement: Engaging the youth in anti-corruption efforts is essential for building a culture of integrity and accountability among future leaders.

30. Public Awareness: Raising public awareness about the negative impacts of corruption and the importance of good governance can foster a sense

of civic responsibility and support for anti-corruption initiatives.

Efforts to combat corruption and improve governance in Gabon are ongoing. These challenges are complex and require sustained commitment and multi-faceted strategies to address effectively. Addressing corruption and strengthening governance is crucial for sustainable development, economic growth, and political stability in the country.

Chapter 4

The Coup D'état

-How did the coup happened

The presidential results were announced 30th August 2023 early Wednesday morning with President Ali Bongo winning the election again. But a few hours later, the situation took a twist with the military announcing a take over.

The address came moments after the national election authority said Bongo had won a third term in Saturday's election with 64.27 percent of the vote.

The mutiny soldiers announced the disssolution of the government including crucial institutions.

The group's members were drawn from the gendarme, the republican guard and other elements of the security forces.

According to the results issued prior to the officers' announcement, Bongo's main rival Albert Ondo Ossa won just 30.77 percent of the vote.

Internet was reportedly restored in Gabon after military officers said they'd taken power.

The private intelligence firm Ambrey said all operations at the country's main port in Libreville had been halted, with authorities refusing to grant permission for vessels to leave. It wasn't immediately clear if airlines were operating in the country.

French mining group Eramet says Gabon activities 'stopped'

First coup in central Africa if successful

Gabon is one of the richest countries in Africa in terms of per capita GDP due largely to its oil revenue and relatively small population of 2.3 million.

Ali Bongo has been seen as a close ally to France. There has been a wave of coup in the west African countries like Burkina Faso, Mali and the latest being Gabon. This is the first coup in the central African region in recent years.

In his annual Independence Day speech Aug. 17, Bongo said "While our continent has been shaken in recent weeks by violent crises, rest assured that I will never allow you and our country Gabon to be hostages to attempts at destabilization. Never."

Overthrowing Mr Bongo would end his family's 56-year hold on power in Gabon.

Unlike Niger and two other West African countries run by military juntas, Gabon hasn't been wracked by jihadi violence and had been seen as relatively stable.

The economic ans social situation has left many disillusioned though. Nearly 40% of Gabonese ages 15-24 were out of work in 2020, according to the World Bank.

Gabon is a member of the OPEC oil cartel, with a production of some 181,000 barrels of crude a day, making it the eighth-largest producer of oil in sub-Saharan Africa.

At a time when anti-French dominance is spreading in many former colonies, the French-educated Bongo met President Emmanuel Macron in Paris in late June and shared photos of them shaking hands. France has some 400 troops in in the country.

A military coup thrust the Central African nation of Gabon into turmoil Wednesday, unseating the president – whose family had held power for more than half a century – just minutes after he was named the winner of a contested election.

Ousted President Ali Bongo Ondimba, also known as Ali Bongo, has faced accusations of election fraud and corruption since he began ruling the oil-rich but poverty-stricken nation nearly 14 years ago. Following the coup, residents in the country's capital were seen celebrating and embracing soldiers on the street.

But much remains uncertain, with Bongo reportedly under house arrest, his son arrested, all borders closed and the government ostensibly shut down. International leaders have expressed concern and condemnation of the coup, some warning their citizens in Gabon to shelter in place.

Here's what you need to know.

How did the coup happen?
The military's power grab began Wednesday, shortly after Gabon's election authority said Bongo had been re-elected president following last weekend's election.

Men in army uniforms announced on national television that they had seized power. They said the election results were voided, all borders shut, and numerous government bodies dissolved, including both houses of parliament.

The coup leaders said Bongo had been placed under house arrest, surrounded by "family and doctors." The ousted president's son, Noureddin Bongo Valentin, was arrested alongside six others for "high treason."

A video aired by the Agence France-Presse news agency shows Bongo seated in what looks like a library, saying he was "at the residence" and didn't know what was happening. "My son is somewhere, my wife is another place," he said.

It was not immediately clear under what circumstances the clip was filmed.x

Meanwhile, the junta named Gen. Brice Oligui Nguema – who was once the bodyguard of Bongo's late father, the previous ruler of Gabon – as a transitional leader.

Speaking to French newspaper Le Monde on Wednesday, Oligui claimed Bongo was enjoying "all his rights" as a "normal Gabonese" citizen.

Conclusion

The junta later announced the arrest and home detention of Bongo and his eldest son and adviser Noureddin Bongo Valentin adding that the two were with family and doctors. However, lawyers for Ali Bongo's wife Sylvia Valentin later claimed that Nouredin was being held in an undisclosed location. The President of the National Assembly, Richard Auguste Onouviet, was also arrested by the junta, along with presidential chief of staff Ian Ghislain Ngoulou, his deputy Mohamed Ali Saliou, presidential spokesperson Jessye Ella Ekogha , another presidential adviser and the two top officials in Bongo's Gabonese Democratic Party (PDG). The junta said that they were arrested on charges that included treason, embezzlement, corruption, falsifying the president's signature and drug-trafficking. Trunks, suitcases and bags filled with billions of Central African CFA francs were reportedly seized from their homes, with Ngoulou claiming that some of the money was part of Bongo's election fund.]

Despite his detention, Bongo released a video on social media in which he appeared distressed while pleading for help in English, claiming that he was being held separately from his family while calling on his friends and supporters both in Gabon and around the world to "raise their voice" and "make noise" in response to the coup.Following his appeal, the CEO of a communications firm that helped Bongo during the election said that the military seized the phones of those who were with Bongo